From
Pride
to
Humility

A Biblical Perspective

Revised Edition

Stuart Scott

From
Pride
to
Humility

It is probably safe to say that humility is the one character quality that will enable us to be all Christ wants us to be. We cannot come to God without it. We cannot love God supremely without it. We cannot be an effective witness for Christ without it. We cannot love and serve others without it. We cannot lead in a godly way without it. We cannot communicate properly without it. We cannot resolve conflict without it. We cannot deal with the sin of others rightly without it. We especially cannot resist sin without it. In short, we must embrace and live out humility in order to truly live and be who God means for us to be. It is for this reason that God exhorts us through Paul:

> **Therefore I, the prisoner of the Lord, implore you to walk in a manner worthy of the calling with which you have been called, with all humility and gentleness.... .**
> **Ephesians 4:1-2**

The Enemy of Humility: Pride

You cannot have humility where pride exists. Pride is the opposite of humility and it is one of the most loathed sins in God's sight.

> **Everyone who is proud in heart is an abomination to the Lord; assuredly, he will not be unpunished.**
> **Proverbs 16:5**

Pride is the epidemic vice. It is everywhere and manifests itself in many ways. As much as we may hate to admit it, we all have pride, each and every one of us. The question is not, "Do I have it?" but, "Where is it?" and "How much of it do I have?" We all have the tendency to think too much *about* ourselves and too much of ourselves. Amy Carmichael once said, "Those who think too much of themselves don't think enough." Pride is evidence of foolishness and childishness. Charles Swindoll said, "The world's smallest package is a man wrapped up in himself." Here is what God says about the proud person:

> **Do you see a man wise in his own eyes?**
> **There is more hope for a fool than for him.**
> **Proverbs 26:12**

Andrew Murray said that pride is "the root of every sin and evil." (Andrew Murray, *Humility*, Springdale, PA, Whitaker House, 1982, p.10.) Murray is right—pride is the beginning of every sin. Despite the fact that it is so widespread, it is perplexing how little has been written on pride in recent years. To read very much on the subject of pride, one must read Puritan literature.

Throughout the Scriptures you see the pride of position (Matthew 23:6), ability (2 Chronicles 26:15-16), achievement (Daniel 4:22), wealth (1 Timothy 6:17), possessions (Matthew 6:19), knowledge (Isaiah 47:10), learning (1 Corinthians 8:1), spiritual attainment (Luke 22:24), self-righteousness (Romans 10:3), being esteemed or liked (Galatians 1:10), and even pride of spiritual experiences (2 Corinthians 12:7). Our flesh has a bent toward pride. Pride is an easy snare for the devil to use. The Puritan Thomas Watson said, "It is a spiritual drunkenness; it flies up like wine into the brain and intoxicates it. It is idolatry; a proud man is a self-worshiper" Some people try to hide their pride behind spiritual words and actions, but it is there nonetheless.

Some Biblical Terms

Six different Hebrew words are used for pride. All of them convey lifting up, highness, magnification, presumptuousness, or rebelliousness of self. In the Greek language, the words for pride occur in two different categories. One particular word group suggests the idea of "straining or stretching one's neck" (as if to hold one's head up high because of what one thinks he has made of himself or accomplished), "to magnify," or "to be haughty". The other category in the Greek conveys a "blindness" and even suggests the idea of being "enveloped with smoke." Throughout the Scriptures, in both the Greek and Hebrew languages, we find proud people portrayed as having a high view of themselves. While they are "up there" on high in their own thinking, they are blind! They are blinded to their pride, they are blinded to God's truth and, sometimes, even blinded to simple reality. The great Puritan Richard Baxter said, "... [pride is] so undiscerned by the most, that it is commonly cherished while it is commonly spoke against" Biblical synonyms for pride are: vainglory, conceit, boasting, arrogance, loftiness, presumption, haughtiness, being puffed up, high-mindedness, scoffing, and self-seeking.

Some Biblical Examples

We never find the Scriptures saying, "Come on now, you're thinking too poorly of yourself" or "What you need is to

3

consider yourself more." Instead, God has given us many stories and warnings to discourage this very thing. In essence, Scripture tells us to stop focusing on ourselves or on what we want. Illustration after illustration of pride appears in Scripture. The best example of the sin of pride is that of Satan. He voiced the mindset of every proud person when he questioned and denied God (Genesis 3:1-5). Uzziah served God for many years, growing prosperous, famous, and strong, "but when he became strong, his heart was so proud that he acted corruptly" (2 Chronicles 26:16). Nebuchadnezzar's arrogance ruined his life, until he humbled himself before the Most High, praising the One who "is able to humble those who walk in pride" (Daniel 4:37). Belshazzar failed to learn his father's lesson, exalting himself, rather than God, and was destroyed for his pride (Daniel 5:18-30). The Pharisee in Luke 18:10-14 ended up praying only to himself because he considered himself so superior and righteous. Other biblical examples of men who were ruined by their pride include King Saul (1 Samuel 18:7-9), King Herod (Acts 12), and Diotrephes (3 John 9).

We have been given many warnings about the desire to lift up self and serve self. It is also the natural inclination of pride to forget about God or want to be above God. God has been faithful to address the destructive sin of pride with verses like:

> **Pride goes before destruction, and a haughty spirit before stumbling.**
> **Proverbs 16:18**

> **Do nothing from selfishness or empty conceit, but with humility of mind regard one another as more important than yourselves; do not merely look out for your own personal interests, but also for the interests of others.**
> **Philippians 2:3-4**

A Definition of Pride

When someone is proud they are focused on self. This is a form of self-worship. A person is prideful who believes that they, in and of themselves, are or should be the *source* of what is good, right and worthy of praise. They, also believe that they, by themselves, are (or should be) the *accomplisher* of anything that is worthwhile to accomplish, and that they should certainly be the *benefactor* of all things. In essence, they are believing that all things should be *from* them, *through* them, and *to* them or *for* them. Pride is competitive toward others, and especially toward God. Pride wants to be on top. Thomas Watson is quoted to have said, "Pride seeks to ungod God." This phrase certainly describes the arrogant.

But what about those who are caught up in self-pity, who are self-absorbed with a sense of failure? This too is pride. They are just on the flip side of the pride "coin." People who are consumed with self-pity are focusing on their own selves too much. They are not concerned with the glory of God and with being thankful for what good gifts and talents the Lord has given them, but instead are focused on how they think they have gotten a "raw deal," or how they are not "as good as" someone else. Self-pitying people desperately *want* to be good, not for the glory of God, but for themselves. They *want* to do things for and by their own power and might for the personal recognition. They *want* everyone to serve them, like them, and approve of them. When these desires are not fulfilled, a prideful person will become even more inwardly focused and will continue a vicious cycle. The self-focused person who bemoans the fact that they are *not* what they desperately want to be (elevated and esteemed) should not be deceived by thinking they are not proud. Nothing could be further from the truth. To sum it all up, a proud person believes that life is all about *them*—their happiness, their accomplishments, and their worth. From our study we can put together a definition of pride that will help us evaluate our own desires and practices. Pride is:

The mindset of self (a master's mindset rather than that of a servant): a focus on self and the service of self, a pursuit of self-recognition and self-exaltation, and a desire to control and use all things for self.

Manifestations of Pride

As we have said, pride is blinding. This fact is why it is often difficult to see pride in ourselves, and yet so easy to see it in others. Here is a sample list of pride manifestations that can easily clear away the smoke of any self-righteousness.

1. *Complaining against or passing judgment on God.* A proud person in a difficult situation thinks, "Look what God has done to *me after all* I have done *for Him*" (Numbers 14:1-4, 9,11; Romans 9:20).

2. *A lack of gratitude in general.* Proud people usually think they deserve what is good. The result is, they see no reason to be thankful for what they receive. As a matter of fact, they may even complain because they think they deserve better. They tend to be critical, complaining and discontent. The proud person is not in the practice of being thankful toward God or others (2 Chronicles 32:25).

3. *Anger.* A proud person is often an angry person. One's anger can include outbursts of anger, withdrawing, pouting, or frustration. Another word for anger is moody. An angry look has been called, "silent murder". A person most often becomes angry because his "rights" or expectations are not being met (Matthew 20:1-16).

4. *Seeing yourself as better than others.* A proud person is usually on top looking down on others. He gets easily disgusted and has little tolerance for differences (Luke 7:36-50).

5. *Having an inflated view of your importance, gifts and abilities.* Many proud people have a very wrong perception of themselves. They are a legend in their own mind, but what they really need is a loving dose of reality. They need to hear, "What do you have that God didn't give you?" (1 Corinthians 4:7).

6. *Being focused on the lack of your gifts and abilities.* Some proud people may not come across proud at all, because they are always down on themselves. This is still evidence of pride because one is focused on self and wants self to be elevated. Having a "woe is me" attitude is self-pity, which is pride (1 Corinthians 12:14-25).

7. *Perfectionism.* People who strive for everything to be perfect often do so for recognition. They may do it so they can feel good about themselves. Whatever the reason, this behavior is very self-serving and proud. The basic problem is making things that are less important, more important (Matthew 23:24-28).

8. *Talking too much.* Proud people who talk too much often do it because they think that what they have to say is more important than what anyone else has to say. When there are many words, sin is generally unavoidable (Proverbs 10:19).

9. *Talking too much about yourself.* A person who is proud may center on themselves in conversation. Sharing personal accomplishments and good personal qualities with others can be bragging or boasting (Proverbs 27:2; Galatians 6:3).

10. *Seeking independence or control.* Some proud people find it extremely difficult to work under someone else or to submit to an authority. They have to be their own boss. They might say, "I don't need anyone," or "I don't need accountability for my faith and doctrine." They are often rigid, stubborn, headstrong, and intimidating. They may also say, "It's my way or no way" (1 Corinthians 1: 10-13; Ephesians 5:21).

11. *Being consumed with what others think.* Some proud people are too concerned about the opinion of others. Many of their decisions are based on what others might think. Some are in a continual pursuit of gaining the approval and esteem of others. Focusing on what others think of you or trying to impress others is being a man-pleaser rather than a God-pleaser (Galatians 1:10).

12. *Being devastated or angered by criticism.* Proud people usually struggle a great deal with criticism. Such people cannot bear that they are not perfect or have weaknesses because they cannot accept who they really are (Proverbs 13:1).

13. *Being unteachable.* Many proud individuals know it all. They're superior. They can't seem to learn anything from someone else. They respect no one (Proverbs 19:20; John 9:13-34).

14. *Being sarcastic, hurtful, or degrading.* Proud people can be very unkind people. Those who belittle other people usually want to raise themselves up above others. Very often this can be quite cleverly done through jesting. They may excuse themselves by saying, "That's just the way I am. That's my personality" (Proverbs 12:18, 23).

15. *A lack of service.* Proud people may not serve because they are not thinking of others, or because they want to be coaxed to serve and don't want to continue if there is no praise. Needing recognition is a sure sign of the wrong motives in service (Galatians 5:13; Ephesians 2:10).

16. *A lack of compassion.* A person who is proud is rarely concerned for others and their concerns. They cannot see beyond their own desires (Matthew 5:7; 18:23-35).

17. *Being defensive or blame-shifting.* You will often hear a proud person say, "Are you saying it's *my* fault?" or "Well, what about you?" They try to explain away their sin. (Genesis 3:12-13; Proverbs 12:1).

18. *A lack of admitting when you are wrong.* A proud person will make a great many excuses such as, "I was tired," or "I was having a bad day" (Proverbs 10:17).

19. *A lack of asking forgiveness.* Proud people rarely admit their sin or ask for forgiveness of others. They either cannot see their sin because they are blinded by their pride, or they just can't seem to humble themselves before someone else and ask forgiveness (Matthew 5:23-24).

20. *A lack of biblical prayer.* Most proud people pray very little, if at all. Proud people who do pray usually center their prayers on themselves and their desires, rather than God and others (Luke 18:10-14).

21. *Resisting authority or being disrespectful.* A proud person may detest being told what to do. We might say he or she has a submission problem. What they actually have, however, is a pride problem. It is simply displaying itself in a lack of submission (1 Peter 2:13-17).

22. *Voicing preferences or opinions when not asked.* A proud person might not be able to keep his preferences or opinions to himself. He will offer it when it is not asked for. These preferences are usually voiced without consideration for others (Philippians 2:1-4).

23. *Minimizing your own sin and shortcomings.* A proud person typically believes that their sin is no big deal. They think they have a little sin and others have a great deal of it (Matthew 7:3-5).

24. *Maximizing others' sin and shortcomings.* To the proud person, other people are the problem. They may magnify or bring attention to the sin of others by gossiping about the other's sin (Matthew 7:3-5; Luke 18:9-14).

25. *Being impatient or irritable with others.* A proud person might be angry with other people because they are concerned that their own schedule or plans are being ruined.

They are often inflexible on preference issues (Ephesians 4:31-32).

26. *Being jealous or envious.* Often when they do not enjoy the same benefits, proud people have a hard time being glad for other's suc-cesses or blessings (1 Corinthians 13:4).

27. *Using others.* The proud person usually views others in terms of what those people can do for *them* and *their* interests. Their focus is not on ministering to others. Everything is *for them* and *about them* (Matthew 7:12; Philippians 2:3-4).

28. *Being deceitful by covering up sins, faults, and mistakes.* Some proud people will do just about anything in order for others not to find out negative things about them (Proverbs 11:3; 28:13).

29. *Using attention-getting tactics.* A proud person may try to draw attention to themselves through dress, bizarre behavior, being rebellious, always talking about their problems, etc. (1 Peter 3:3-4).

30. *Not having close relationships.* Proud people often have no use for close relationships, thinking that the trouble outweighs the benefits. They may see themselves as so self-sufficient that they do not need other people (Proverbs 18:1-2; Hebrews 10:24-25).

Here is a way that we can picture our definition and man-ifestations of pride:

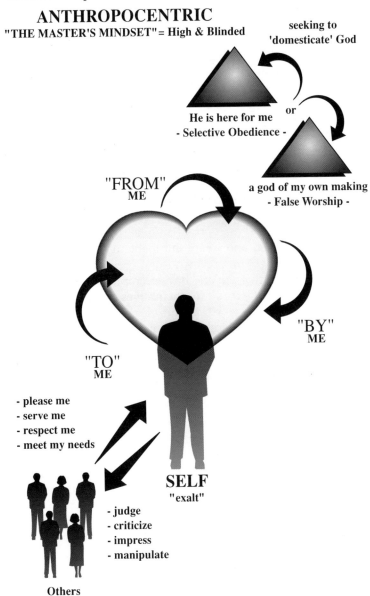

ANTHROPOCENTRIC
"THE MASTER'S MINDSET"= High & Blinded

seeking to
'domesticate' God

He is here for me
- Selective Obedience -

or

a god of my own making
- False Worship -

"FROM"
ME

"BY"
ME

"TO"
ME

- please me
- serve me
- respect me
- meet my needs

- judge
- criticize
- impress
- manipulate

SELF
"exalt"

Others

All of these perspectives encourage a focus on self and a purposeful lifting up of self. As we will see even more clearly in our later discussion on humility, this self-centeredness is in direct opposition to the biblical perspectives of *lowliness and others-mindedness*. These ideas are surely designed by the evil one and are embraced as good and right by a worldly system. Even many Christians have been deceived by these wrong perspectives. One can be so easily deceived because the basic philosophies behind them are very appealing to the flesh. On the contrary one *can have* a proper view of self without these wrong perspectives. An appropriate view begins by seeing oneself rightly in reference to God and others and involves voluntary humility towards both for the right reasons.

What is an appropriate view of self? We are so very far beneath God and totally unworthy before Him (Psalm 8:1-4). We are no better and no worse than others, because we are all desperately wicked and totally incapable of anything worthwhile in God's sight on our own (John 15:5; Romans 3:10-18). There is nothing that anyone has accomplished or possesses that they should take credit for themselves (1 Corinthians 4:7). We basically have no worth in and of ourselves, but God has given us (believers) a place we do not deserve and has set His love on us anyway (Ephesians 2:4-7). God has rightly and wisely given everyone an allotment of ability that is to be used for His glory and for the purposes He has planned (Ephesians 2:10; Peter 4:10).

We *are* low in comparison to God. This is why we serve *Him* with a *lowly* mindset. We are told to *voluntarily place* ourselves lower than others because God has declared humility a virtue. This is why we serve *others* with a *lowly* mindset. When we fully embrace who we really are and live as God has commanded, we will have a proper view of self. We will *not* be focused on self *in any way*. Instead, we will be God-and others-focused. Those who have been involved with the unbiblical perspectives mentioned above should confess any manifestation of self-focus as the sin of pride.

Linger a Little Longer

Once we begin to recognize pride in our own life we may want to move on too quickly. It is of the utmost importance to see pride for what it really is and to understand just how deeply it runs in our lives. We must say the same thing God says about it, confess it, and truly repent. We must acknowledge it as the abomination to God that it is and we must humble ourselves before a holy and just God.

The life of Job is a good illustration of our own need to do more than just recognize pride. Job reaches a point in his trials where he begins to question and judge God. But God presses Job with questions that lower Job to his rightful place and exalt God in Job's mind and eyes (Job 38-41). Halfway through, God says, "Will the faultfinder contend with the Almighty?" (Job 40:1a). Interestingly Job says, "Behold, I am insignificant; what can I reply to you? I lay my hand on my mouth" (Job 40:3-4). At this point we might think, "Good, you got the message, Job. Now we can move on to the rest of the story." Instead, Job needed to linger in the presence of God a little longer, in order for his pride to be fully exposed. In essence the Lord says, "I'm not through with you yet, Job. I have a few more questions." God then goes on for two more chapters. By the end, Job doesn't just say, "I lay my hand on my mouth." He says,

> **"I know that you can do all things, and that no purpose of Yours can be thwarted. Who is this that hides counsel without knowledge? Therefore I have declared that which I did not understand, things too wonderful for me, which I did not know. "Hear now, and I will speak; I will ask You, and You instruct me. I have heard of You by the hearing of the ear; but now my eyes see You; therefore I retract, and I repent in dust and ashes."**
> **Job 42:2-6**

Job's thinking now is quite different from just recognizing his pride. Job has moved from simply being silenced to full acknowledgement of who God is, and humble repentance of his lack of exalting God rightly. Job is now going in the opposite direction, giving glory to God and seeing himself rightly. We too have to be sure that we don't move on too quickly when we think we recognize pride in our lives. I am not suggesting a never-ending inward search or morbid introspection. Dr. Martyn Lloyd-Jones has said:

> I suggest that we cross the line from self-examination to introspection when, in a sense, we do nothing but examine ourselves, and when such self-examination becomes the main and chief end in our life. We are meant to examine ourselves periodically, but if we are always doing it, always, as it were, putting our soul on a plate and dissecting it, that is introspection. And if we are always talking to people about ourselves and our problems and troubles, and if we are forever going to them with that kind of frown upon our face and saying: I am in great difficulty – it probably means that we are all the time centered upon ourselves. That is introspection, and that in turn leads to the condition known as morbidity (*Spiritual Depression*, Wm. B. Eerdmans Publishing Company, Grand Rapids, Michigan, 1965, p. 17).

The first step to true repentance is seeing pride for what it really is. The second step is to put on humility. Let's explore what true humility is.

The Attribute of Humility

If pride is the epidemic vice, then humility is the endangered virtue. Humility is so rare because it is unnatural to man. Only a Christian who has the Spirit of God can learn genuine humility. The more we learn humility, the more our lives will change. Just as pride is the root of every evil, humility is the root of every virtue.

There are several Old Testament terms translated *humility* or *humble*. Mostly they refer to the action of *bowing low* or *crouching down*. This is what we should do in our hearts. In the New Testament, there are two words used, one meaning *servile, base* or *groveling* and the other meaning *gentle, meek* or *yielding*. These attitudes were very negative concepts in the Greek culture, but Christ revealed them to be virtues.

Our Greatest Example

Of all the biblical examples of humility, the greatest by far is the example of Christ Himself. Christ's very coming to earth was an amazing act of humility. Try to imagine what Christ had in heaven—glory, honor, pure worship and majesty. Then read in Philippians how He humbled Himself:

> **Who, although He existed in the form of God, did not regard equality with God a thing to be grasped, but emptied Himself, taking the form of a bond-servant, and being made in the likeness of men... He humbled Himself by becoming obedient to the point of death, even death on a cross.**
> **Philippians 2:6-8**

Jesus described himself as "meek and lowly in heart" (Matthew 11:29, KJV). Certainly, He knew when to be firm and when to rebuke others for God's glory (Matthew 23), but He was truly humble of heart. While Christ was here on earth, He was in complete submission to the Father's will, even though He Himself was God (John 4:34; 8:28-29). He was devoted to glorifying God (John 17:1, 4). Christ became the servant of men and taught His disciples to do the same (John 13:3-17):

> **"For even the Son of Man did not come to be served, but to serve, and to give His life a ransom for many."**
> **Mark 10:45**

Jesus' perspective is very different from the thinking people often have. In our society, the *first* or the one who is lifted up is the greatest. According to Jesus, however, the *least* is the greatest. The humblest person is the greatest person of all (Mark 10: 43-44). This means that the proud person is last in God's eyes. Jesus' life is just the opposite of what is valued today. God's Word tells us that we must have the perspective of Christ, rather than that of the world (Romans 12:2).

One of Christ's greatest displays of humility was, of course, His act of washing the disciples' feet (John 13:1-17). Though He was God, He wrapped the servant's towel around His waist and cleaned the dirt and perspiration off men's feet. You would think that one could not get any lower than that. And yet, Christ's most amazing demonstration of humility and service was the suffering and death He endured on behalf of sinners like you and me. Since Almighty God was willing to stoop so low and serve mankind in life and in death, we should, therefore, be willing to place ourselves below others. Let's pick up the towel and the basin!

Other Biblical Examples

Other examples of humility in Scripture abound. Abraham gave Lot the first choice when they parted company and divided the land (Genesis 13). Moses is said to be "more humble than anyone else on the face of the earth" (Numbers 12:3). John the Baptist acknowledged that he was not worthy to untie Christ's sandals (Luke 3:16). Mary, the mother of Jesus, submitted herself completely to God's will saying, "Behold the bondslave of the Lord; may it be done to me according to Your word" and "My soul exalts the Lord ... for He has had regard for the humble state of His bondslave" (Luke 1:38, 46, 48). The tax collector beat his breast and prayed, "God, be merciful to me, the sinner" (Luke 18:13). The Apostle Paul was one of the greatest New Testament examples of humility. He told the Ephesian elders, "I was ... serving the Lord with all humility and with tears" (Acts 20:18-19). Paul also referred to himself as, the "chief" of sinners, and the "least of all saints" (1 Timothy 1:15 KJV; Ephesians 3:8). Paul had a right perspective of who he was in respect to God. He said:

> **Oh, the depth of the riches both of the wisdom and knowledge of God! How unsearchable are His judgments and unfathomable His ways! For who has known the mind of the Lord, or who became His counselor? Or who has first given to Him that it might be paid back to him again? For from Him and through Him and to Him are all things. To Him be the glory forever. Amen.**
> **Romans 11:33-36**

A Definition of Humility

When someone is humble they are focused on God and others, not self. Even their focus on others is out of a desire to love and glorify God. They have no need to be recognized or approved. There is no competition with God or others. They have no need to elevate self, knowing that they have been forgiven and that God's love has been undeservedly and irrevocably set on them. Instead, a humble person's goal is to elevate God and encourage others. In short, they "no longer live for themselves, but for Him who died and rose again on their behalf" (2 Corinthians 5:15). From these truths we can put together a simple definition of humility:

The mindset of Christ (a servant's mindset): a focus on God and others, a pursuit of the recognition and the exaltation of God, and a desire to glorify and please God in all things and by all things He has given.

Manifestations of Humility

A humble person lives differently than a proud one. How does your life measure up in the area of humility? Here is a sample list to help you evaluate how humble you are.

1. *Recognizing and trusting God's character.* A humble person acknowledges Who God is and rehearses God's character often. Because he does this, he trusts God much more than the proud person. In trials, he will even thank God for the reminder of how much he needs Him and for all the good He is doing through the trial (Psalm 119:66).

2. *Seeing yourself as having no right to question or judge an Almighty and Perfect God.* A humble man thinks of God as his Creator and himself as God's creation. He does not see himself as even remotely qualified to pass judgement on God or what God does. He knows that his perfect and all-wise God can do whatever He pleases, and it will be the best for him (Psalm 145:17; Romans 9:19-23).

3. *Focusing on Christ.* The humble see Christ as their life and their first love. There is no other thing or person that they must have. Through the day they talk to and worship Him often (Philippians 1:21; Hebrews 12:1-2).

4. *Biblical praying and a great deal of it.* Humble people want to worship God and they see themselves as totally dependent on God for His enablement. John Owen once said, "We can have no power from Christ unless we live in a persuasion

that we have none of our own." Because they see themselves as needy, they pray often (1 Thessalonians 5:17; 1 Timothy 2:1-2).

5. *Being overwhelmed with God's undeserved grace and goodness.* The humble person sees himself as truly deserving of hell. He is immensely grateful to God for forgiving him of so much (Psalm 116:12-19).

6. *Being thankful and grateful in general toward others.* Humble people thank God and others often. They expect nothing, so anything that is received is greatly appreciated. (1 Thessalonians 5:18).

7. *Being gentle and patient.* Humble people want to act like God, and they are not focused on what they want. They also want to love others the way God loves them. They are willing to wait and are not easily irritated (Colossians 3:12-14).

8. *Seeing yourself as no better than others.* A humble person understands the sinfulness of his own heart. He would never see himself as better than others. This is true no matter who the other person is. He understands that he, in and of himself, is capable of the worst sin. He agrees with John Bradford who said, "but for the grace of God, there I go" (Romans 12:16; Ephesians 3:8).

9. *Having an accurate view of your gifts and abilities.* Humble people do not bemoan the fact that they are not as gifted as others. Neither do they exaggerate their own abilities (Romans 12:3).

10. *Being a good listener.* Humble people consider what others have to say as more important than what they have to say. They take an interest in others by asking questions and listening. Self is not their primary focus (James 1:19; Philippians 2:3-4).

11. *Talking about others only if it is good or for their good.* A humble person will speak well of others, not negatively. He will convey something negative about someone only if he must do so in order to help that person (Proverbs 11:13).

12. *Being gladly submissive and obedient to those in authority.* Humble people are first of all obedient to God, and then the authorities over them (Romans 12:1-2; 13:1-2).

13. *Preferring others over yourself.* Humble people are willing to put others before self without first considering their own rights (Romans 12:10).

14. *Being thankful for criticism or reproof.* Humble people view reproof as good for them and consider that God may be trying to teach them something (Proverbs 9:8; 27:5-6).

15. *Having a teachable spirit.* Humble people realize they don't know everything, and even when they think they are right are willing to consider that they might be wrong (1 Corinthians 4:7). They also know that God can use anyone to teach them, since He was even able to use a donkey to teach Balaam in Numbers 22:22-35. They have many people they admire and respect.

16. *Seeking always to build up others.* Humble people encourage others. They use only words that build up and say what is necessary for the edification of others. They never cut others down (Ephesians 4:29).

17. *Serving.* Humble people are on the lookout for ways to serve and assist others. They are the first to volunteer for jobs no one else wants. They take the initiative to reach out and serve others (Galatians 5:13).

18. *A quickness in admitting when you are wrong.* Humble people have no problem with saying, "I was wrong. You are right. Thank you for telling me." (Proverbs 29:23).

19. *A quickness in granting and asking for forgiveness.* Humble people are eager to forgive because they know how much they have been forgiven. They have no trouble asking for forgiveness because they want to be peacemakers (Colossians 3:12-14).

20. *Repenting of sin as a way of life.* A humble person asks God daily for forgiveness and works toward real change (1 John 1:9; 1 Timothy 4:7-9).

21. *Minimizing others' sins or shortcomings in comparison to your own.* A humble person thinks about his own sin more often than another's sin. He also sees his own sin as more important to deal with than the sin of others (Matthew 7:3-4).

22. *Being genuinely glad for others.* Humble people rejoice with others when good things happen because they are aware that God has blessed them immeasurably and they trust God for what they do not have (Romans 12:15).

23. *Being honest and open about who they are and the areas in which they need growth.* Humble people are open and honest about their growth in the Lord. They ask for help and accountability in the repentance process, knowing they need their brothers and sisters (Philippians 3:12-14; Galatians 6:2).

24. *Possessing close relationships.* Humble people have friends and loved ones because they are friendly and love others They are willing to ask for help with various burdens and problems they may have. (Acts 20:31-38).

Here is a way that we can picture our definition and manifestations of humility:

THEOCENTRIC
"the SERVANT'S MINDSET" = Low & Sober-Minded

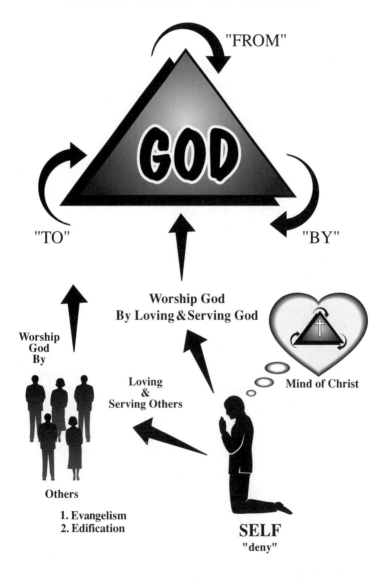

Getting from Here to There

So how do we get from pride to humility? First of all there must be an initial humbling of one's self before God. We are told in the New Testament:

> **Submit therefore to God. Resist the devil and he will flee from you. Draw near to God and He will draw near to you. Cleanse your hands, you sinners; and purify your hearts, you double-minded. Be miserable and mourn and weep; let your laughter be turned into mourning and your joy to gloom. Humble yourselves in the presence of the Lord, and He will exalt you.**
> **James 4:7-10**

Without humility there can be no true repentance (change). In other words we have to humble ourselves before God and then we can *walk* in humbleness. It takes humility to learn humility. That initial humbling of one's self is a response to the work of the Spirit of God. Once we have rightly humbled ourselves before God there are things that we can do (by God's grace) to stay humble.

To remain humble:

1. Pray for God to help you put off pride and to produce humility in you.
2. Read the Psalms and the Prophets often to gain a high view of God and proper self view.
3. Study Jesus (His earthly examples; especially in the Gospels).
4. Ask others if you come across as proud in any way.
5. Spend lots of time worshiping God (e.g. praising, prayer, reading and meditating).
6. Practice the "one-another" principles (Appendix 3).
7. Work to put off pride and put on humility at the level of your thoughts and motives.
8. Work to put off pride and put on humility at the level of your communication.
9. Work to put off pride and put on humility at the level of your deeds.

10. Have the mindset that humility must be a way of life (Plilippians 2:3).

Before we conclude, let's review by way of a chart what we have learned thus far:

ATTITUDE	PRIDE	HUMILITY
Outlook:	Epidemic	Endangered
Terms:	High, Lifted Up, Blind	Low, Bowed Down, Sober
Mindset: (attitude of)	Self: The Master	Jesus Christ: The Servant
Source of Good:	From Me	From God
Means of Good:	By/Through Me	By/Through God
Goal of Good:	To Me	To God
Honor:	Self-Imposed	God-Bestowed
Confidence:	Self-Sufficient	Christ-Sufficient
Others:	Conditional/Trading Affection (looked down upon)	Unconditional/Sacrificial (preferred) • Salvation • Sanctification

Get Humble and Keep Humble

It should be abundantly clear that without humility we cannot be the exemplary Christians God has called us to be. In turn, one cannot put on humility if he doesn't first realize areas where he has sinful pride. Pride lies behind every sin and especially behind strife and contention (Proverbs 13:10).

We just saw in James that "God is opposed to the proud" (James 4:6). God is actively fighting against pride in order that He might capture or win us (Ezekiel 14). Earlier, in this same passage, James says, "He jealously desires the Spirit which He has made to dwell in us" (James 4:5). Christian, God will deal with your pride if you will not. He will do this because He loves you and because He made you to glorify Him. Spurgeon believed that "every Christian has a choice between being humble or being humbled."

To the humble God promises grace (James 4:6). John MacArthur says, "Humility creates the vacuum that divine grace fills." When we see ourselves rightly in reference to God and others, we will shine with God's glory. Paul tells us in Colossians, "As those who have been chosen of God, holy and beloved, put on a heart of ... humility ..." (Colossians 3:12). This putting on of humility, unfortunately, is not a one-time thing. Pride does not die once, but it must die daily. The Puritan pastor, Thomas Brooks, admonished us well when he said, "Get humble and keep humble."

> **For thus says the high and exalted One who lives forever, whose name is Holy, "I dwell on a high and holy place, and also with the contrite and lowly of spirit, in order to revive the spirit of the lowly, and to revive the heart of the contrite.**
>
> **Isaiah 57:15**

Notes